Chilterns Scene

First published in Great Britain in 1993 by Toby & Charlie Books
The Bell Bookshop
Bell Street
Henley on Thames
Oxfordshire

Photographed and produced by Chris Andrews, Oxford
Text by Fiona Danks
Edited by David Huelin
Designed by Mike Brain

ISBN 0 9520993 0 6

Printed in Hong Kong

Front cover
Ewelme

Back cover
Marlow   Princess Risborough
Henley
Wallingford   West Wycombe

Chilterns Scene

Photographed by Chris Andrews

Toby & Charlie Books

CONTENTS

Introduction	5
Wallingford	14
Shillingford	18
Ewelme	20
Swyncombe	28
South Stoke	30
Moulsford	34
Goring	36
Wargrave	44
Shiplake	46
Henley-on-Thames	48
Mill End	60
Hambleden	62
Crays Pond	66
Stoke Row	68
Nettlebed	70
Bix Bottom	72
Greys Court	74
Medmenham	76
Marlow	78
Pishill	82
Stonor	88
Turville	96
Turville Heath	102
Fingest	104
Skirmett & Frieth	110
West Wycombe	114
Bradenham	120
Watlington	124
Chinnor	126
Thame	128
Princes Risborough	136
Monks Risborough	138
Beech Woods and the Furniture Industry	140
Lanes, Footpaths & the M40	146
Maps	156
Index	158

INTRODUCTION

The Chiltern Hills, though they are near London and are crossed by several major roads, remain remarkably unspoilt and tranquil. This is a secret landscape, much of its beauty only becoming apparent when one looks for it;

> compared to, say, the Cotswolds or the South Downs, it is an unknown country, and you can drive across its 400 square miles on one of the major through roads and barely realise you have been there.

This quotation from Richard Mabey's *Home Country* could describe the journey through the Chilterns driving from London on the M40 where you may barely be aware that there are a few valleys and some distant views. It is only as the road suddenly plunges down through the escarpment between vertical cliffs of chalk that a dramatic vista over the countryside below is revealed and you realise that you must have missed something. To find the real Chilterns you must leave the main roads and take to the narrow winding lanes or some of the 1500 miles of well marked footpaths. There you will find rolling chalk hills with hidden, steep-sided valleys, cathedral-like beech woods, rich chalk grasslands and picturesque villages with brick and flint cottages.

The Chiltern Hills begin at the Goring Gap in Oxfordshire and extend 50 miles north-east to Deacon Hill near Hitchin in Hertfordshire. This prized part of the English landscape was designated an Area of Outstanding Natural Beauty (AONB) in 1965, which gave some degree of protection to these chalk hills and their unspoilt villages. This book provides a glimpse of some of the towns, villages and countryside of the southern Chilterns.

The name Chiltern is perhaps best explained by this quotation from Camden in his *Britannia* of 1695;

> Chiltern hath its name from the soil, cyle or chilt, a Saxon term signifying chalk, for it riseth for the most part in chalky hills, covered in woods and groves of beech.

This outcrop of chalk on the north west rim of the London basin was laid down about 100 million years ago when the area was covered by a warm shallow sea. The calcium carbonate skeletons of microscopic creatures accumulated on the sea floor over a very long period to produce thick layers of chalk. Some 74 million years later the continental plates of Africa and Europe collided, causing much buckling and folding in both continents. One result of this was the tilting of the chalk strata now making up the Chilterns, creating a

The Thames South of Henley.

steep scarp slope and a dip slope with a gradient so imperceptible that it resembles a plateau. Overlying this chalk plateau are other materials such as clay with flints and sand and gravel, also deposited when the area was under the sea and now capping much of the higher ground.

The landscape we see today has been created out of these raw materials by the slow process of weathering and erosion. The most imposing feature is the escarpment, often 50 metres or more above the foothills, with its series of prominent hills overlooking the Oxfordshire plain. Behind the scarp is the dip slope, dissected by an irregular pattern of mostly dry valleys, a characteristic feature of chalk topography, probably eroded by the meltwater from glaciers that reached the escarpment during one of the Ice Ages. In some places the valleys lie close together divided by narrow ridges commanding views over each side; in other places the ridges are so wide that they resemble plateaux. One other significant feature is the Thames, bordering parts of the southern Chilterns and separating them from the Berkshire Downs where it flows through the Goring Gap.

It is probably not the shape of the land that typifies this area so much as the vegetation covering it. This is one of the most richly wooded landscapes in England with almost twenty percent of its area tree-covered; the towering beech trees, with their smooth straight trunks standing above an almost bare woodland floor, present the most familiar image of Chiltern woods. There are several types of both broad-leaved and coniferous woodland, much of it found on hill-tops or clinging to steep valley sides. It is on these steeper gradients with their poor, shallow soils that remnants of the once extensive unimproved chalk grassland are found, with aromatic herbs, rare orchids and clouds of butterflies. On some of the ridges areas of heath dominated by oak, birch and bracken grow on the acidic sandy soils, in contrast to the flora of the more alkaline chalk. Any easily accessible land with better soil is farmed; most of it is arable land but there is some livestock production, including a few outdoor pigs kept in open fields. Despite the unspoilt countryside there is a surprisingly large human population living in numerous small villages in the heart of the Chilterns and in towns on the periphery of the hills or in the larger valleys.

The area has changed since people first began to clear the primeval forest that covered it. The original woodland was probably dominated by oak, ash and wych elm, but when clearance began in the Neolithic period (4000 - 2000 BC) beech began to get a foothold, its shallow, spreading root system well suited to the thin dry soils. The oldest signs of human habitation are various scatters of flint implements and the Whiteleaf long barrow on the escarpment near Princes Risborough. The Icknield Way, thought to have been a pathway since Neolithic times, follows a route below the summit of the hills; once an important route linking East Anglia with the south coast, the Icknield Way is now a footpath.

After the Roman invasion of Britain there followed four centuries of highly civilised development; the Chiltern region was governed from Verulamium, now St Albans. Much land was cleared for cultivation and there is evidence to suggest that villas were built in many of the valleys, although only one has been verified. After the collapse of Roman rule in the fourth century much of the cultivated land reverted to woodland during the Dark Ages. The most significant landmark from this period is Grim's Ditch, a long earthwork boundary, which can be seen in several places. With the spread of Christianity the Saxons began to build churches, traces of which remain despite the fact that rebuilding by the Normans destroyed most of the Saxons' work.

Looking over Grim's Ditch.

Beech wood North of Bradenham.

At the time of Domesday in 1086, settlement was mostly in scattered farmsteads and hamlets, and woodland cover was far greater than it is now. Beech trees were already widespread at that time and many were probably planted for pannage, the fattening of swine on beech mast. Domesday quotes pannage returns for many Chiltern manors; for example 6,615 acres of woodland at Hambleden would support 700 hogs whereas 2,420 acres at Medmenham only supported 50.

From as early as the tenth century many counties were divided into administrative units known as "hundreds"; although these have long since disappeared, the office of "Steward of the Chiltern Hundreds" still exists. Throughout the Middle Ages the Chiltern Hundreds were the haunt of highwaymen and thieves making it an unsafe place for travellers, particularly on the important route to Oxford and the north. The Steward, first appointed by the Normans, was required to ride the forests and catch any criminals he could find; today the post is less onerous, providing an easy income for a retiring Member of Parliament.

During the Middle Ages the area was managed by several landed families among them the Stonors of Stonor, the de Greys of Rotherfield and the Blounts of Mapledurham. The indiscriminate clearance of woodland declined in the thirteenth century as it was found to be an increasingly valuable resource. Woodlands that had previously been common land used by tenants for fuel and grazing were now enclosed by the lords of the manors, to be used for hunting and coppiced for charcoal and other woodland products. Timber and firewood from the southern end of the Chilterns were shipped to London down the Thames, which had been an important transport route for centuries. In some ways the Chilterns have changed little since medieval times when there were scattered farms and villages, mixed farming for crops and a large amount of woodland cover. The similarity can be seen because there has been a continued reliance on forestry and agriculture with very little industrial development and few entirely new settlements.

Much of the settlement pattern can be explained by water, or lack of it, for the high porosity of chalk means that there is very little surface water in the Chilterns. Early settlement was near the Thames, in the bottoms of the main valleys and on the scarp foothills near the spring line created where the chalk overlies less permeable rock. Villages that grew up on the ridges relied on wells or clay-lined ponds, many of which can still be seen today. The local building material used since the Middle Ages is flint, but the corners of buildings and the door and window surrounds must be made of stone or brick as flint cannot "turn a corner". Most of the older buildings are roofed with tiles, some made from local iron clay.

From the beginning of the sixteenth century farming in the hills was predominantly a sheep-corn husbandry while the woodlands were managed on a coppicing system to provide fuel. Products not used locally were sent to London, the river remaining a major transport link until the development of the railways in the nineteenth century. As coal became more widely available there was less demand for firewood but a new market for timber was emerging with the developing furniture industry. The landscape of the Chilterns owes much to this industry, which is described in a separate section.

The twentieth century has brought rapid change and greatly improved transport links bringing the Chilterns closer to London and other large towns. Many of the villages appear unchanged, but a closer look reveals that to some degree the region has become a dormitory, a quiet but accessible retreat for commuters. There have been many changes since people working in London were first

Brick and flint at Monks Risborough.

enticed to "come and live in Metroland" in the 1930s when the first estates were built. The growth of light industry and suburban housing in and around the towns, and the crude ribbon development of several ridge-top villages, may seem insensitive, but this is not a museum and some growth is inevitable. Perhaps the most significant changes in the landscape are the transport links, in particular the M40 which, unlike other major routes, does not follow a large valley but slices through the escarpment and over the dip slope. The rural economy still relies heavily on forestry and on mixed arable farming; intensified production led to the loss of many hedgerows, but in more recent times large areas of arable land have been put into "Set aside" in an effort to reduce crop surpluses. Sheep grazing is no longer common but there is now greater demand for horse pasture.

There is much for the resident and the visitor to enjoy in the Chilterns, from visiting picturesque villages and old houses to walking the well-marked footpaths, exploring the many nature reserves and enjoying the old inns. With their rich landscape and flora the Chilterns have long been recognised as an area worthy of protection; since 1965 the Chiltern Society, a voluntary organisation, has worked to conserve and enhance the area. The Society's interests are many and varied but perhaps its most obvious contribution has been the clear marking of all the rights of way so that walkers and horse riders can make use of the many paths and bridleways. Several long distance trails follow and traverse the Chilterns, including the Ridgeway, the Oxfordshire Way and Swan's Way.

The diverse natural history is protected in many nature reserves belonging to the National Trust, English Nature, and the Berkshire Buckinghamshire and Oxfordshire Naturalists' Trust, the Local Wildlife Trust. Although the tall beech woods with their bare floors are an impressive and majestic sight they are not so interesting to the naturalists, who prefer the mixed woodlands where there is more light and hence a richer ground flora. These woods are a delight in spring with their primroses, wood sorrel and yellow archangel. There are several remnants of chalk grassland, the product of years of continuous grazing by sheep and rabbits. During the summer months these carpets of wild flowers include such species as marjoram, wild thyme, birdsfoot trefoil and orchids. The rich vegetation of the area supports many species of vertebrates, bird and mammal; deer can often be seen from the quieter lanes and footpaths.

Red kites have occasionally been seen here; these extremely rare birds were once widespread but the only wild population in Britain is restricted to a small area in Wales. There is now a programme to re-introduce the red kite to southern England; several pairs have been released at secret locations and these huge birds with their forked tails have been seen soaring over the Chilterns. Perhaps they will find enough space and natural habitat to live and breed here again, giving their seal of approval to the beautiful landscape.

A steep-sided valley South of Lane End.

Poppy fields at Piddington.

Rape fields near Goring.

WALLINGFORD

The Market Place.

The Thames was once quite easily fordable here, providing a crossing since Roman times or earlier. The first reference to a bridge in Wallingford is 1141; the present bridge dates from the thirteenth century but has been altered. Of its seventeen arches only five span the river itself.

The original Saxon town was destroyed in 1006 by the Danes. In 1066 William the Conqueror crossed the river here and a year later he commissioned Robert D'Oilley to build a castle. The Empress Maud took refuge here in 1142 and in 1420 Henry V presented the castle to his bride Catherine de Valois as a wedding gift. In the Civil War it was sacked by Cromwell's army as Wallingford was the last Royalist stronghold in the County. Only a few crumbling walls remain, most of the stone having been used elsewhere.

Nowadays Wallingford is a busy town with narrow streets and a charming market place overlooked by the pillared seventeenth century town hall.

Wallingford Bridge and the spire of St Peter's Church.

In a local orchard.

The centre of the town from the castle ruins.

An early nineteenth-century bridge crosses the river at Shillingford. There are some old houses near this pretty stretch of the river, one of which, Shillingford Court, was the home of Lillie Langtry.

The Thames below Shillingford Bridge.

EWELME

Rooftops and the church.

Ewelme is situated in a valley near the foot of the Chilterns, and is one of several spring-line settlements in the area. Its name means "at the source of a stream or spring"; the swiftly flowing water of the brook has been used for growing water-cress for hundreds of years.

Adjoining the church is a group of fifteenth-century almshouses and a school built by Alice Chaucer, grand-daughter of Geoffrey and owner of the manor of Ewelme.

The church contains notable tombs of the Chaucer family, and Jerome K. Jerome, who lived here in more recent times, is buried in the churchyard. The cloister adjacent to the church is one of the oldest brick buildings in this area, and the almshouses are still in use today. Ewelme school, like the almshouses, was founded in 1437 and is the oldest church school in the country.

The village from the South.

Arms on Ewelme School.

Inside the entrance to the almshouses, with the garden beyond.

Courtyard of the fifteenth-century almshouses with the old well.

Mr C. W. Bray of Ewelme with a successful day's catch.

St Mary's Church.

St Botolph's Church.

Near Ewelme is Swyncombe House and a small Norman church dedicated to Saint Botolph. For many years the church was connected with the Abbey of Bec in Normandy; in 1203 the monks there were awarded the right to hold an annual fair at Swyncombe for Saint Botolph's day, June 17th. A fair took place each year until some time in the nineteenth century when the incumbent Priest decided it was a "profanity of the Lord's Day".

Swyncombe is an old English name meaning "pig valley" probably referring to the hunting of wild boar when the estate had more woodland than it has today. The area is still quite wooded but there are open grasslands with the clumps of trees typical of parkland. At one time the estate was over 1000 acres with a large mansion and numerous outbuildings and cottages. The original Elizabethan house was destroyed by fire and replaced about 1840.

The village from the South East.

SOUTH STOKE

A village house.

South Stoke lies upriver from Goring between the Great Western Railway and the Thames, with the Berkshire Downs to the west and a rather bleak intensively farmed area of the Chilterns to the east.

This is an attractive village with a local population; there are many old houses and a thirteenth century church much altered in the fourteenth century. Next to the church is a farm which was once part of a monastery; the orchard, full of apple blossom in the spring, is dominated by a magnificent dovecote, said to be the largest cruciform dovecote in the country.

The Ridgeway goes through the village and along a narrow lane down to the river where a ferry once crossed to the Beetle and Wedge at Moulsford. This inn is said to have inspired H.G. Wells to write *The History of Mr Polly.*

The cruciform Dovecote.

The thirteenth-century Church of St Andrew.

Brick patterns in a (slightly) newer construction.

Directly across the river from South Stoke is Moulsford.

The Beetle and Wedge at Moulsford with a restored Oxford college barge.

GORING

The lock in summer.

Goring marks the western limit of the Chiltern Hills where the Thames flows through the Goring Gap, separating the Chilterns from the Berkshire Downs. The river was first crossed here by a branch of the Icknield Way; later a causeway was built by the Romans to be followed by another ford, a ferry, a toll bridge, and in 1923 the present bridge.

Goring, in its attractive setting and with a Great Western Railway station, became popular at the beginning of this century, when elaborate boat-houses and Edwardian mansions were built. The heart of the town has retained its character with many old brick and flint buildings. Views over the lock and weir make it a popular place with visitors and it is a favourite stopping place for boaters, particularly as it is one of only a few places to offer free 24-hour mooring.

The church was originally the chapel of a nunnery founded here in 1135 by Henry I; it has been much altered but still has its Norman tower.

The lock and weir with the village behind. In the foreground Streatley on the western bank.

Not all Goring's properties have been renovated.

The Norman tower of Goring Church overlooking the old mill pond and moorings.

Pay and Display.

Inside the Leatherne Bottel – formerly a riverside pub, now a noted restaurant.

On the outskirts of Goring, rape fields leading to the hills.

An original Thames camping skiff.

WARGRAVE

Regatta Fireworks.

Strictly speaking Wargrave is on the wrong side of the Thames to be included in this book but its proximity to Henley and its situation at the foot of a steep chalk ridge gives it the feel of a Chiltern village. At the time of Domesday Wargrave was one of the richest and most populous settlements in East Berkshire. Originally called Weirgrove this settlement remained a rural community until the end of the nineteenth century. Nowadays it is a busy village, and its position on the river has made it popular. Overlooking the village is Wargrave Manor, an imposing white mansion built about 1780 and now owned by the Sultan of Oman.

With Shiplake lock a short distance upstream near where the Loddon joins the Thames there is much activity on the river here. For many years there was a ferry to take passengers to the field on the other bank where a track leads to Shiplake; nowadays this service only operates during Wargrave's regatta held in August.

The Sultan of Oman's personal band at the regatta.

Moored just up the Lodden, electric boats at the annual rally, held at differing places near Henley.

A different sort of boat, human powered at the regatta races.

The riverside.

A settlement was first established at this river crossing in the twelfth century. Henley has always been a busy place with good transport links; for many years it was a port supplying timber, corn and malt to London. In the eighteenth century it was an important coaching post, and with the coming of the Great Western Railway in 1857 Henley grew still further. Now it is an affluent commuter town.

Beside the majestic eighteenth century bridge is the Angel pub, held by Cromwell's men during the Civil War. The Red Lion once gave lodgings to Charles I; and Prince Rupert is said to have hanged a spy on a tree known as "Rupert's Elm". At the Old Brewery the long-standing industry of malting is still carried on.

Looking over the Thames to Henley with the resident swans.

Temple Island, originally an Edwardian retreat, now hired for hospitality during the regatta.

The Angel and eighteenth-century bridge with the distinctively patterned church behind.

Bell Street, Christmas Eve.

Brakspear's Henley Brewery.

HENLEY ROYAL REGATTA

Pre-race training.

Henley is perhaps best known for its Royal Regatta, a major social event that takes over the town for the 27th week of each year. Rowing crews come from all over the world to race along possibly the best stretch of river in Britain. In 1829 the first boat race between Oxford and Cambridge took place here; ten years later Henley launched its annual regatta. Prince Albert became the first patron in 1851 and the regatta acquired its Royal prefix.

The first regatta was over in three hours; today preparations for the event start in April and the races are on five days of July followed by a week's art and music festival. There are striking contrasts between the competing crews and the formally dressed guests. For the majority of people this colourful pageant has more to do with champagne and strawberries than physical prowess and the river.

Weather at the regatta is variable.

Looking up the course, a mile and a quarter straight stretch of river.

The atmosphere of the regatta is made by the racing, and other attractions.

The arts and music (and dining) festival that follows the regatta.

MILL END

The weir curtain on the Thames.

The small village of Mill End stands near Hambleden lock and weir; the remains of a Roman villa were found here in 1911. It is believed there were other such villas in the Chilterns, but this is the only one discovered and excavated; the objects unearthed are in Aylesbury Museum.

To the west of the village is Greenlands, the Victorian home of W.H. Smith (1825-1891), who developed a small news-agency into a large business. He also reached high office in government and is said to have been the gentleman in *HMS Pinafore* who "never went to sea and rose to be the ruler of the Queen's Navy". The Greenlands estate, and much of the village of Hambleden, was given to the National Trust in 1944.

Riverside houses in summer.

The village shop and Post Office.

The village of Hambleden stands beside the river Hamble, one of few rivers in the Chilterns. Built almost entirely of brick and flint, its cottages huddle round the church, forming a scene that has changed little over the years. This village is perhaps more modest than some Chiltern villages; it is protected by the National Trust, and external alterations can only be made with their permission.

Hambleden is associated with several famous names. The Earl of Cardigan, leader of the Charge of the Light Brigade, was born here; so too was Thomas de Cantalupe, the medieval saint. Buried in the churchyard are W. H. Smith and Major George Howson, who set disabled World War veterans to work making poppies.

A pastoral scene, the village from the South.

View over the churchyard to the backs of village cottages.

The Bakery, now producing less perishable goods.

CRAYS POND

A small settlement south of Stoke Row.

Local woodland walks.

STOKE ROW

The Maharajah's Well.

Surrounded by beech woods on a ridge of the Chilterns is the linear village of Stoke Row. The church of St John the Evangelist may look like a thirteenth century building but is only about 150 years old. The village still has many old houses, particularly near the small green.

Visitors to the village may be surprised to see the oriental well dating from 1863, which along with the adjacent cottage and orchard is a charitable trust endowed by the Maharajah of Benares. This unlikely gift came about through a local man Edward Reade, Governor of the North West Provinces of India in the nineteenth century. While carrying out a water scheme in Benares he became acquainted with the local Maharajah, who was distressed to hear that villagers in the Chilterns suffered from severe water shortage in the summer months. The Maharajah subsequently donated funds to sink a well here in Stoke Row, to ensure that the village would always have sufficient water.

Autumn, the village playing fields.

The kiln

Nettlebed is situated on a clay-and-flint-capped ridge and villagers here used the clay to make bricks and pottery; although the use of flints was common in much of the Chilterns, clay seems not to have been so widely employed. The earliest references to a kiln in Nettlebed are the accounts for 35,000 tiles made for Wallingford Castle in 1365 and for 200,000 bricks for Stonor Park in 1416. By the mid nineteenth century an extensive brickworks had replaced the scrub and woodland of Nettlebed Common.

All that remains now are some clay pits and one kiln, surrounded by new houses. On the main road are the iron gates leading to Joyce Grove, a "Jacobethan" mansion built in 1904 for the Fleming family. Later Joyce Grove was the home of Ian Fleming, creator of James Bond, and his brother Robert, soldier, explorer, author and husband of actress Celia Johnson. Robert and Celia returned to live in this area and both lie buried here. Joyce Grove is now a Sue Ryder Home.

Joyce Grove, once home to the creator of James Bond.

GREYS COURT

The Manor House.

Not far from the small village of Rotherfield Greys is the old manor house Greys Court, home of the de Greys family at the time of Domesday and for the succeeding four centuries. In the sixteenth century King Henry VIII gave the fortified manor and its estate to his friend Francis Knollys, who later became a Counsellor to Queen Elizabeth. When the Queen visited him here, she entered through a gatehouse he had built for the occasion.

Among the extensive outbuildings is the largest surviving example of a donkey wheel, used until 1914. A donkey trod the inner slatted surface of a large wheel to pull water up from a 200 foot well. The informal gardens are set amongst the ruins of the original manor. The brick-paved maze was laid out in 1980; it is based on the pavement maze at Chartres Cathedral. The house and grounds were given to the National Trust in 1969.

The Maze.

MEDMENHAM

The Abbey Tower.

For hundreds of years two ferries crossed the Thames at Medmenham, reduced to one in 1851 with river traffic in decline in favour of the rapidly developing railway. An impressive memorial on the river bank records the court of appeal decision in 1936 obliging owners of this land to maintain an efficient ferry service; the memorial remains but the ferry has gone.

An Iron Age hill fort and a Cistercian abbey are parts of Medmenham's colourful history. The abbey was founded in the early thirteenth century;

it was always a small and struggling community and like many other monasteries it fell into decline in the late 1400s. Little of the original abbey remains; even the "ruined tower" dates from the eighteenth century when Sir Francis Dashwood altered the Elizabethan house built where the abbey once stood. His "Hell Fire Club" whose members called themselves "Franciscans", used to meet here and there are many stories about their riotous behaviour.

Wisteria—covered house on the lane leading to the river.

The bridge and All Saints Church.

Marlow's attractive setting on the Thames, not far from the wooded hills, has made it popular with writers. The poet Shelley lived in West Street for several months with his wife Mary, author of *Frankenstein*. West Street was also home to T. S. Eliot in 1918 and the poet Thomas Love Peacock in early 1800. Jerome K. Jerome lived above the town on Marlow Common and parts of his book *Three Men in a Boat* were written in the Two Brewers pub.

The suspension bridge built in 1831 is by William Tierney Clark, who later designed the great suspension bridge between Buda and Pest.

The town has several buildings of note including Remantz in West Street where the lavish stable block is thought to have been designed by Wren. The Royal Military College occupied this building from 1799 until 1811 when it moved to more spacious quarters at Sandhurst.

Marlow has its own international regatta in the week before the more famous one in Henley.

'Messing about in boats'.

View of the church over the weir pool.

On the river.

PISHILL

The village pub.

This small hamlet situated in a steep, dry valley consists of a cluster of houses and a small church upon the hillside. The name, pronounced "Pishhill", originates in the Anglo-Saxon "peas-hill" which suggests that its soil was unsuitable for other crops.

The nineteenth century church replaces a plain Norman predecessor, first mentioned in 1146 when it came under the jurisdiction of Dorchester Abbey. The Stonor estate took over patronage of the church from about 1600 until the mid-nineteenth century, and members of the family are buried here. The south-west window representing a sword and gospel was designed by John Piper in 1967.

Bank Farm, situated just off the road, is a traditional brick and flint cottage painted pink, thanks to the photographer Norman Parkinson who lived here, wilfully mispronouncing the village's name. After several years here he moved to the Caribbean to work and to perfect a sausage recipe.

The nineteenth-century church.

Looking towards Stonor from Pishill.

Autumn on the road from Pishill to Henley.

Arable land between Pishill and Stonor.

Pasture land between Pishill and Stonor.

STONOR

Stonor Park.

This small village lies in a valley near the entrance to Stonor Park where the Stonor family have lived for over 800 years. The house cannot be seen from the gates for it is concealed in a fold in the hillside. The house and adjacent chapel originate from about 1280 but have been much altered; the mellow brick facade was added in the early fifteenth century using bricks from the Nettlebed kilns. The house is open to the public at specified times in the summer.

The Stonor family prospered until about 1570 when, despite the Reformation, they continued to follow the Roman Catholic faith. For over 150 years they led a secret life; they hid priests in the roof, their home became a national centre for Catholic thought and policy and they built up a unique collection of illegally printed recusant books, which is still in the library. The chapel here is one of only three in England where Mass has been celebrated regularly since before the Reformation.

The Stonor Park estate.

Stonor from the estate.

Farm buildings at Stonor.

At Stonor Farm.

Deer in Stonor Park.

Stonor sits virtually on the county boundary.

The Church of St Mary the Virgin.

Turville lies in a quiet valley reached from Northend along Holloway Lane, a steep narrow road reminiscent of a tunnel as it passes between high banks under a canopy of beech trees.

The heart of the village is a small green surrounded by pretty cottages and the church, overlooked by Ibstone Smock Mill high upon the hillside. The mill, whose name describes its smock-like form, ceased working in 1910 and is now a private house, featured in the film *Chitty Chitty Bang Bang*.

The church dates from the twelfth century although the squat tower was added in 1340. As you enter the building you are faced by the brilliant blue of the stained glass window designed by John Piper. Under the tower is a six-foot coffin hewn from a single stone, discovered during restoration work in 1901. It contained not one but two bodies; that of a man probably buried about 700 years ago and a sixteenth-century woman's body with a hole driven through the skull.

The John Piper window.

The village green with the 'smock' mill in the distance.

Looking south over Turville valley.

The Vicarage

Between Turville and Fingest.

TURVILLE HEATH

The hamlet of Turville Heath stands on a ridge to the west of Turville.
Two eighteenth-century houses and a few cottages are hidden among trees of a typical ridge-top heath-land dominated by oak, birch, and bracken.

The village green is overlooked by interesting trees and few houses.

The eastern edge of the village.

Fingest, Turville, Skirmett and Frieth—they roll off the tongue like an ancient nursery rhyme. The name of this village derives from "pinghyrst", meaning a "meeting place in a wood". Fingest is at the meeting of four valleys but much of the surrounding woodland was cleared long ago.

The Norman church has a massive tower with an unusual eighteenth century twin saddleback roof. The interior has an atmosphere of stark simplicity, retaining many of its original features such as the medieval beams and trusses of its high pitched roof.

A notice at the entrance of the churchyard compares great events in world history with this church's progress over the centuries, but it omits the tale of the eighteenth century priest who used the bells as a stake in a wager, losing all but one of them to the village of Hambleden.

Side roads show a variety of architectural styles.

View from the East of the village.

Looking over the churchyard to the pub.

Old grain store raised to ensure flow of air and protection from vermin.

St Bartholomew's Church from the path to Turville.

SKIRMETT & FRIETH

Winter view at Skirmett looking to the hills.

At the source of the river Hamble lies the village of Skirmett, a linear settlement with no church but two pubs. Despite its being such a small place there is a great range of architectural styles from the seventeenth century up to the present day.

A narrow winding lane climbs the steep hill out of Skirmett towards Frieth affording some superb views over Hambleden valley. At the top of the hill and descending the other side is the sprawling village of Frieth, parts of which are almost suburban. The small Victorian church was built in 1848 from flints carted from the ruined wing of the Old Rectory in Hambleden. Most of the woodwork in the church was made by a local firm that specialised in making church furniture from 1869 to 1940, providing local employment.

On the road from the village.

Virginia creeper on a house in Frieth.

The lich-gate at Frieth.

WEST WYCOMBE

West Wycombe Park.

This village is located in the Wye valley beneath West Wycombe Hill, once the site of an Iron Age fort and now dominated by St Lawrence's Church with its imposing golden ball. The Royal Society of Arts bought West Wycombe from the Dashwood family in 1929 wishing to preserve it as a "fine picture of English life and history", an apt description of its main street. The village is now in the care of the National Trust which ensures that there is little unwanted modern development.

Sir Francis Dashwood (1708-1781), dilettante, politician and patron of classical architecture, was responsible for the church and adjacent mausoleum and for the rebuilding of West Wycombe Park in Palladian style. The Park remains the Dashwood family home and is open to the public. West Wycombe caves are a popular attraction, their entrance guarded by a mock ruin; they were excavated by Francis Dashwood to provide chalk to build the long, straight road to High Wycombe.

View down Church Lane.

The Church Loft, a fifteenth-century resthouse for pilgrims.

The golden ball of St Lawrence's Church on West Wycombe Hill.

The George and Dragon yard. The eighteenth-century inn is reputedly haunted by a young woman's ghost.

West Wycombe caves used by the Hell Fire Club.

B R A D E N H A M

The Manor House.

Bradenham is a corruption of three Saxon words, "Broad-dene-ham" meaning a home in a broad valley. In the woodland to the north of the village is a particularly well preserved section of Grim's Ditch, a rampart and ditch probably built as a Saxon boundary.

Much of this delightful village clustered round a large open green is now in the care of the National Trust, along with over 1000 acres of the surrounding countryside. The seventeenth-century Manor House was the home of Isaac Disraeli, who moved here about 1817 when his son Benjamin was 13 years old. The Manor's formal seventeenth-century garden, a rare survival from that time, is being restored by the National Trust.

In 1566 Queen Elizabeth I was entertained at Bradenham Manor; evidence of her visit can still be seen in the "Queen's Gap", a dip in the treetops to the northeast, where a road had to be cut from Hampden Manor before the Queen and her entourage could reach Bradenham.

The Parish Church of St Botolph.

The village green.

Cottage front.

WATLINGTON

The Town Hall.

This is a small market town that grew up near a water source below the Chiltern escarpment. Watlington Hill overlooking the town is owned by the National Trust; it has good views over Oxfordshire and varied vegetation including chalk grassland and a dense yew forest.

Watlington, being close to the Icknield Way, was once a far more important place than it is today, even boasting a castle. The medieval centre of the town was near the church, although no remains of it can be seen. In 1655 Thomas Stonor paid for a grammar school to be built here, with the classrooms on the first floor and an open market beneath. Later called the Town Hall, this fine building became the centre of the community.

View from Watlington Hill.

CHINNOR

The cement works.

Chinnor is noticeable from miles away by the white plume of steam issuing from its cement works. Its fourteenth century church houses one of the largest collections of brasses in the county. The town was sacked repeatedly in the Civil War and a fire in 1685 caused great destruction; few older buildings remain, and the village has been much developed.

At the time of the 1851 census Chinnor's most important industry was chair turning, using timber from the nearby woodlands. The products were taken to High Wycombe for assembly. Since the beginning of this century cement has been made here from the mixture of clay and chalk excavated locally.

Overlooking the town is Chinnor Hill, now a nature reserve managed by the Local Wildlife Trust. Two burial mounds were found here, one revealing the weapons of an Anglo-Saxon warrior. Traces of an Iron Age settlement have also been found in this area.

Towards the sunset from Chinnor Hill.

THAME

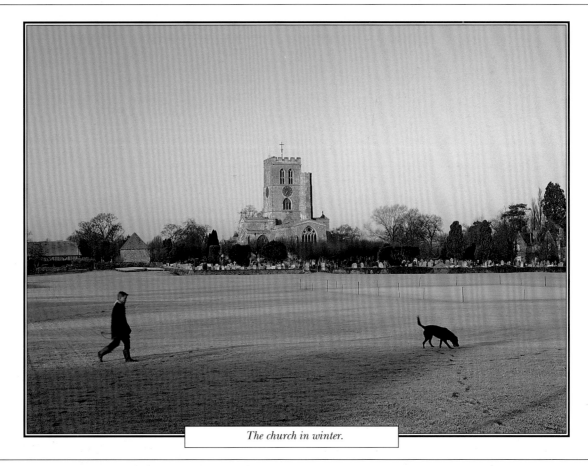

The church in winter.

The old market town of Thame lies a short distance from the hills alongside a river of the same name. The market charter was granted in 1215 and there is a thriving market here, now held every Tuesday. The High Street is of interest for its great variety of architectural styles from different periods. The fifteenth century Birdcage Inn, once a leper-house, was a prison for soldiers during the Napoleonic wars.

The church of St Mary is a light and airy building, its chancel dominated by the imposing alabaster tomb of Lord Williams and his wife. He was a man of wealth and influence, best remembered for the grammar school he established here in the sixteenth century. Pupils at this school have included John Milton, John Wilkes and John Hampden.

The road past the vicarage leading to St Mary's Church.

Carvings in St Mary's Church.

Carvings in St Mary's Church.

The Birdcage (and flower seller).

Town Hall 1887.

Brickwork of the tithe barn near St Mary's Church.

Autumn leaves.

PRINCES RISBOROUGH

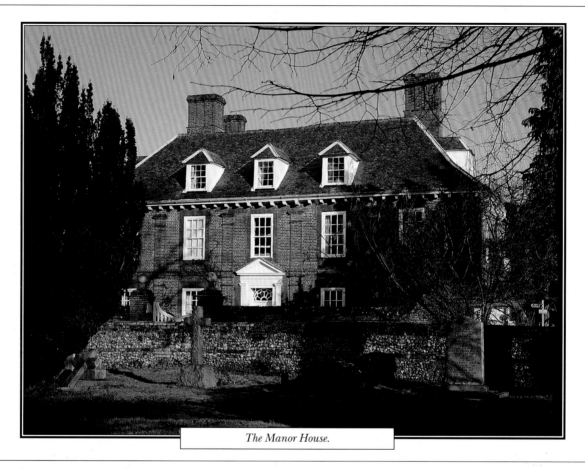

The Manor House.

This small market town retains some of its original character despite being on a direct railway line to London. There are some fine old buildings including timber-framed houses and a seventeenth-century red brick Manor House given to the National Trust by the Rothschilds. The brick market hall with wooden posts below was built in 1824; a regular market is still held on the ground floor.

Princes Risborough is close to a dramatic and historic part of the escarpment; Coombe Hill, at 265 metres the highest point in the Chilterns, is about 2.5 miles or 4 kilometres to the east and several ancient fortifications lie between these two places. Whiteleaf Hill is above the town, its great chalk cross overlooking the Vale of Aylesbury. The origin of this cross remains a mystery; it may have been cut in the seventeenth century or much earlier, but the first undisputed reference to it is in an Act of Parliament in the early nineteenth century commanding that it be cleaned.

St Mary's Church in winter.

Sixteenth-century cottage.

To the north of Princes Risborough is the smaller settlement of Monks Risborough; its largely suburban appearance conceals the unspoilt heart of the village, where sixteenth-century cottages cluster round the church. It was a rural community until the railway came in 1929.

The parish claims to have the earliest surviving certified boundary, dating from AD 903. There has been a church on the site since the parish was created, but the St Dunstan's Church of today is largely of the nineteenth century.

In the village playing fields, close to the church, there is a sixteenth-century stone dovecote.

Dovecote.

BEECH WOODS AND THE FURNITURE INDUSTRY

For many people the Chiltern Hills summon up images of beech woods, perhaps with the fresh, delicate green shades of spring or the rich golden colours of autumn. Yet the glorious, cathedral-like stands of beech are relatively recent; they were planted for the furniture industry which became important in the nineteenth century. When craftsmen began to make furniture here they relied upon the old coppiced woodlands originally used for firewood; as the industry grew, more timber was required and stands of beech were planted.

Beech first became popular in the mid-seventeenth century as a wood for furniture. The Chiltern furniture industry, based around High Wycombe, was particularly associated with the Windsor chair, the first kind of chair to be made widely available to cottagers.

During the eighteenth century demand for chairs grew and a rural industry grew up round High Wycombe, much of the work being done by outworkers known as bodgers. First recorded about 1700, bodgers lived in shacks in the woods where they worked in pairs, felling trees and cutting them into planks in saw-pits. Bodgers' pits can still be seen in some of the woods today. Smaller trees were made into legs and spindles using primitive pole-lathes; these products were sold in High Wycombe where the chairs were assembled in the workshops that grew up all over the town. By 1900 there were more than 100 workshops and factories, mostly producing chairs. High Wycombe is still a centre of the furniture industry but production is now limited to a few larger factories, and there are no longer any bodgers.

Windsor Chairs at the High Wycombe Chair Museum.

Spring, South of Lane End.

Footpath on Watlington Hill.

Winter in the woods outside Henley.

LANES, FOOTPATHS
AND THE M40

Many of the roads and lanes in the southern Chilterns are hidden, following the contours and screened by woods or hedgerows; only the M40 carves its way through the hills ignoring their character. When this road was first proposed it caused much controversy for it effectively sliced a national nature reserve in two and created a huge scar in the hillside. Thirty years later the scar is now an accepted part of the landscape and many of the motorway embankments support a rich variety of plants and animals undisturbed by man.

The oldest road in the Chilterns, and indeed in the country, is the Icknield Way, made by Neolithic man at least three thousand years ago and later improved by the Romans. Stretches of the Icknield Way are now administered with the Ridgeway long-distance trail which stretches 85 miles from Avebury in Wiltshire to Ivinghoe Beacon near Tring, Hertfordshire. South of Goring the Icknield Way follows the same route as the Ridgeway, but in the Chilterns it goes along the base of the escarpment.

Other long-distance trails include the Oxfordshire Way, which links the Cotswolds with the Chilterns by a route from Bourton-on-the-Water to Henley; and Swan's Way, a long-distance bridle route that follows the Ridgeway from Bledlow to Goring.

The Ridgeway in summer.

M. Brain

The Ridgeway in spring.

The M40 hidden (sometimes) in the folds of the Chilterns.

The motorway at night.

M. Brain

Crossing of the Oxfordshire Way and the Ridgeway near Watlington

The Ridgeway near Nuffield.

The main road near Chinnor.

The road to High Wycombe, laid on chalk dug from West Wycombe caves.

The Chilterns, an Area of Outstanding Natural Beauty, with the Thames as a boundry.

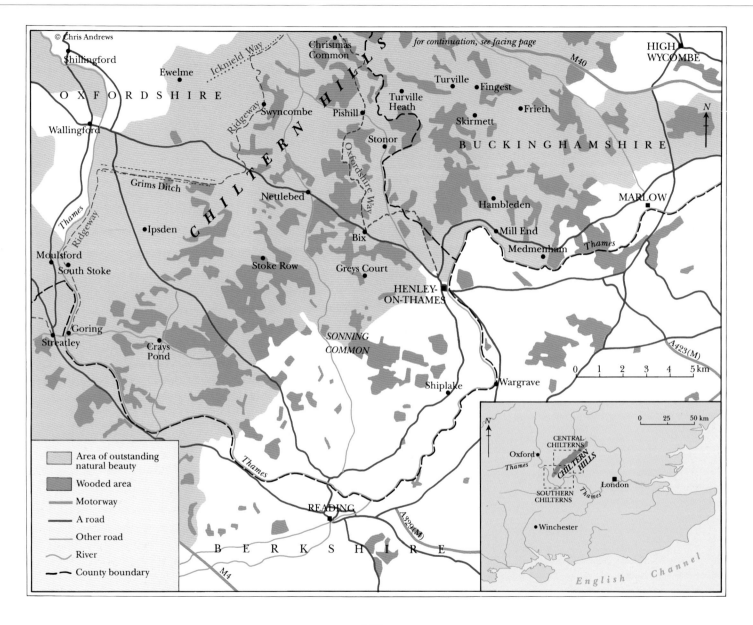

© Chris Andrews

Shillingford

Ewelme

Icknield Way

Christmas Common

for continuation, see facing page

M40

HIGH WYCOMBE

OXFORDSHIRE

Ridgeway

Swyncombe

Pishill

CHILTERN HILLS

Turville

Fingest

Turville Heath

Frieth

Skirmett

BUCKINGHAMSHIRE

N

Wallingford

Stonor

Oxfordshire Way

Grims Ditch

Nettlebed

Hambleden

MARLOW

Thames

Ridgeway

Ipsden

Bix

Mill End

Medmenham

Thames

Moulsford

Stoke Row

Greys Court

South Stoke

HENLEY-ON-THAMES

Goring

Crays Pond

SONNING COMMON

A423(M)

Streatley

0 1 2 3 4 5 km

Shiplake

Wargrave

Thames

Area of outstanding natural beauty

Wooded area

Motorway

A road

Other road

River

County boundary

Thames

READING

A329(M)

B E R K S H I R E

M4

N

0 25 50 km

Oxford

CENTRAL CHILTERNS

Thames

CHILTERN HILLS

London

SOUTHERN CHILTERNS

Thames

Winchester

English Channel

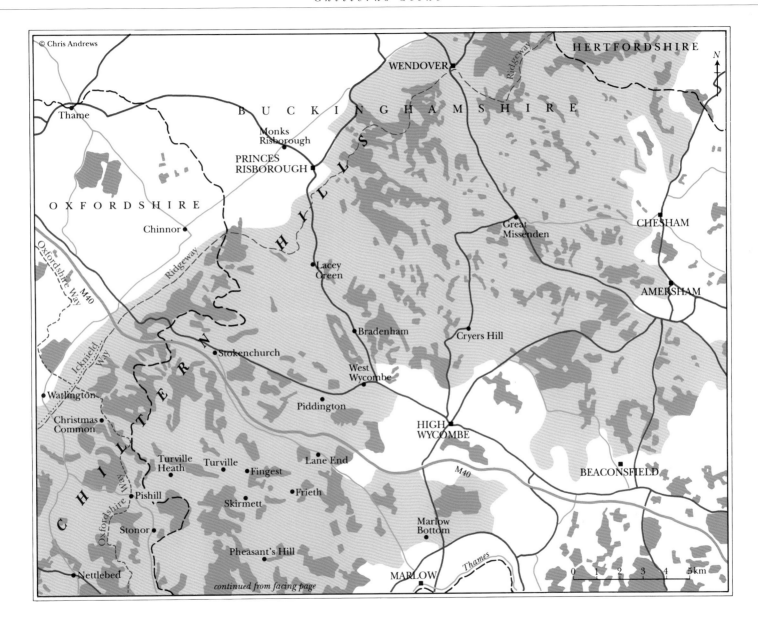

© Chris Andrews

HERTFORDSHIRE

N

Thame

BUCKINGHAMSHIRE

WENDOVER

Ridgeway

Monks
Risborough

PRINCES
RISBOROUGH

H I L L S

CHESHAM

OXFORDSHIRE

Chinnor

Great
Missenden

Oxfordshire Way

Ridgeway

Lacey
Green

AMERSHAM

M40

Icknield Way

Bradenham

Cryers Hill

Stokenchurch

Watlington

West
Wycombe

Christmas
Common

Piddington

HIGH
WYCOMBE

C H I L T E R N

Turville
Heath

Turville

Fingest

Lane End

BEACONSFIELD

Pishill

Frieth

M40

Oxfordshire Way

Skirmett

Stonor

Marlow
Bottom

Pheasant's Hill

Nettlebed

continued from facing page

Thames

MARLOW

0 1 2 3 4 5km

INDEX

Abbey of Bec	28
Albert, Prince	54
Aylesbury, Vale of	136
B.B.O.N.T.	10
Beech Woods	140
Bell Street, Henley	52
Benares, Maharajah of	68
Berkshire Downs	6, 30, 36
Bix Bottom	72
Blounts of Mapledurham	8
Bodgers	140
Bond, James	70
Bradenham	120
Brakspear's Brewery	53
de Cantalupe, Thomas	62
Cambridge	54
Cardigan, Earl of	62
Chalk	5, 7, 9
Charles I	48
Chartres Cathedral	74
Chaucer	20
Chiltern Hundreds	8
Chiltern Society	10
Chinnor	126
Chitty Chitty Bang Bang	96
Civil War	14, 48, 126
Clarke, William Tierney	78
Clay	9
Coombe Hill	136
Crays Pond	66
Cromwell	14, 48
Dark Ages	7
Dashwood, Sir Francis	76, 114
Deacon Hill	5
Disraeli, Isaac, Benjamin	120
Domesday	8, 44
East Anglia	7
Eliot, T. S.	78
Elizabeth, Queen	74, 120
English Nature	10
Ewelme	20
Fingest	104
Fleming, Ian, Robert	70
Flint	6, 9
Footpaths	146
Frieth	110, 112
Furniture Industry	140
Goring	36
Goring Gap	5, 6, 36
Gravel	6
Great Western Railway	30, 36, 48
Greys Court	74
de Greys of Rotherfield	8
Grim's Ditch	7, 120
Hambleden	8, 62, 104, 110
Hampden, John	128
Hell Fire Club	76
Henley on Thames	48
Henley Festival	59
Henley Royal Regatta	54
Henry I	36
Henry V	14
Henry VIII	74
High Wycombe	114, 140
Howson, Major George	62
Ibstone	96
Ice Age	6
Icknield Way	7, 36, 124, 146

Iron Age	126	Piper, John	82, 96, 97
		Pishill	82
Jerome, Jerome K.	20, 78	Princes Risborough	136
Johnson, Celia	70		
		Reade, Edward	68
Knollys, Francis	74	Red Kite	10
		Reformation	88
Lane End	11, 142	Ridgeway	10, 30, 146
Langtry, Lillie	18	River Thames	6, 8, 9, 14, 30, 36, 44, 78
Loddon	44, 46	River Hamble	62, 110
London	8	Roads	146
		Romans	7, 146
M40	5, 10, 146	Rothschilds	136
Mabey, Richard	5	Royal Military College	78
Marlow	78	Royal Society of Arts	114
Marlow Common	78	Rupert, Prince	48
Marlow Regatta	78		
Maud, Empress	14	Churches	
Medmenham	8, 76	St Andrew - South Stoke	32
Middle Ages	8, 9	St Bartholomew - Fingest	109
Mill End	60	St Botolph - Bradenham	121
Milton, John	128	St Botolph - Swyncombe	28
Monks Risborough	138	St Dunstan's - Monks Risborough	138
Moulsford	30, 34	St John the Evangelist- Stoke Row	68
		St Lawrence - West Wycombe	114
National Trust	10, 74, 114, 120, 124, 136	St Mary the Virgin - Turville	96
Nettlebed	70	St Mary's - Ewelme	27
Normans	7, 8	St Mary's - Princes Risborough	137
Northend	96	St Mary's - Thame	128
Nuffield	151	St Peter's - Wallingford	15
		All Saints - Marlow	78
D'Oilley, Robert	14	Goring	36
Oxford	54	Hambleden	62
Oxfordshire Way	10, 146	Pishill	82
		Sand	6
Parkinson, Norman	82	Saxon	5, 7, 120
Peacock, Thomas Love	78	Shelley	78
Piddington	12	Shillingford, Court, Bridge	18

Shiplake	44, 46
Skirmett	110
Smith, W. H.	60, 62
South Stoke	30
St Albans	7
Stoke Row	68
Stone	9
Stonor	88
Stonor, Thomas	124
Stonors of Stonor	8
Streatley	37
Sultan of Oman	44, 45
Swan's Way	10, 146
Swyncombe	28
Temple Island	50
Thame	128
Turville	96
Turville Heath	102
Wallingford	14, 70
Wallingford Bridge	15
Wargrave	44
Wargrave Regatta	44
Watlington	124
Watlington Hill	124, 143
Wells, H. G.	30
West Wycombe	114
West Wycombe Park	114
Whiteleaf Hill	136
Wilkes, John	128
William the Conqueror	14
Williams, Lord	128
Windsor Chair	140, 141
Wye Valley	114